W9-AAT-718

Native American Library

NAVAJO
History and Culture

Helen Dwyer and D. L. Birchfield

Consultant Robert J. Conley
Sequoyah Distinguished Professor at Western Carolina University

Gareth Stevens
Publishing

Pasadena Public Library
1201 Jeff Ginn Memorial Dr
Pasadena, TX 77506-4895

Please visit our website, **www.garethstevens.com**. For a free color catalog of all our high-quality books, call toll free 1-800-542-2595 or fax 1-877-542-2596.

Library of Congress Cataloging-in-Publication Data

Dwyer, Helen.
Navajo history and culture / Helen Dwyer and D. L. Birchfield.
    p. cm. — (Native American library)
Includes index.
ISBN 978-1-4339-6674-3 (pbk.)
ISBN 978-1-4339-6675-0 (6-pack)
ISBN 978-1-4339-6672-9 (library binding)
1. Navajo Indians—History. 2. Navajo Indians—Social life and customs. I. Birchfield, D. L.,
1948- II. Title.
E99.N3D86 2012
979.1004'9726—dc23

                          2011026006

New edition published in 2012 by
Gareth Stevens Publishing
111 East 14th Street, Suite 349
New York, NY 10003

First edition published 2005 by Gareth Stevens Publishing

Copyright © 2012 Gareth Stevens Publishing

Produced by Discovery Books
Project editor: Helen Dwyer
Designer and page production: Sabine Beaupré
Photo researchers: Tom Humphrey and Helen Dwyer
Maps: Stefan Chabluk

Photo credits: AP/Wide World Photos: p.23; Corbis: pp. 10 (bottom), 14 (top),
18 (bottom), 19, 20, 21 (both), 22 (top), 25 (both), 27, 31, 34, 36, 37 (left); Native Stock: pp. 5, 18
(top), 22 (bottom), 26, 30, 33; North Wind Picture Archives: pp. 12, 13 (both), 32; Peter Newark's
American Pictures: pp. 14 (bottom), 16, 17, 24; Shutterstock: pp. 5 (David Watkins), 28 (Paul B.
Moore), 29 top (Linda Brotkorb), 29 bottom (William Attard McCarthy); Wikimedia: pp. 7 (New
York Public Library), 8 (U. S. National Archives), 35 (LeRoy N. Sanchez/Los Alamos National
Laboratory), 37 (Eric Brown/U.S. Navy), 38 (Bill Koplitz/FEMA Photo Library), 39 (Eric S. Garst/
U. S. Navy).

All rights reserved. No part of this book may be reproduced in any form without permission in writing from the publisher, except by a reviewer.

Printed in the United States of America

CPSIA compliance information: Batch #CW12GS: For further information contact Gareth Stevens, New York, New York at 1-800-542-2595.

CONTENTS

Introduction 4

Chapter 1: Land and Origins 10

Chapter 2: History 12

Chapter 3: Traditional Way of Life 20

Chapter 4: Navajo Life Today 30

Chapter 5: Current Navajo Issues 38

Timeline 40

Glossary 42

More Resources 44

Things to Think About and Do 46

Index 47

Words that appear in the glossary are printed in **boldface** type the first time they appear in the text.

INTRODUCTION

The Navajos are a people of Arizona, New Mexico, and Utah in the southwestern United States. They are just one of the many groups of Native Americans who live today in North America. There are well over five hundred Native American tribes in the United States and more than six hundred in Canada. At least three million people in North America consider themselves to be Native Americans. But who are Native Americans, and how do the Navajos fit into the history of North America's native peoples?

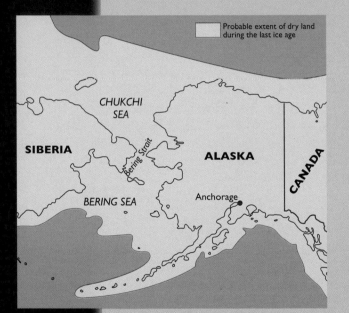

Probable extent of dry land during the last ice age

CHUKCHI SEA

SIBERIA

Bering Strait

ALASKA

CANADA

BERING SEA

Anchorage

Siberia (Asia) and Alaska (North America) are today separated by an area of ocean named the Bering Strait. During the last ice age, the green area on this map was at times dry land. The Asian ancestors of the Navajos walked from one continent to the other.

THE FIRST IMMIGRANTS

Native Americans are people whose **ancestors** settled in North America thousands of years ago. These ancestors probably came from eastern parts of Asia. Their **migrations** probably occurred during cold periods called **ice ages**. At these times, sea levels were much lower than they are now. The area between northeastern Asia and Alaska was dry land, so it was possible to walk between the continents.

Scientists are not sure when these migrations took place, but it must have been more than twelve thousand years ago. Around that time, water levels rose and covered the land between Asia and the Americas. The ancestors of the Navajos and the peoples who spoke similar languages may have been among the last to cross the Bering Strait.

The Cliff Palace at Mesa Verde, Colorado, is the most spectacular example of Native American culture that survives today. It consists of more than 150 rooms and pits built around A.D. 1200 from sandstone blocks.

By around ten thousand years ago, the climate had warmed and was similar to conditions today. The first peoples in North America moved around the continent in small groups, hunting wild animals and collecting a wide variety of plant foods. Gradually these groups spread out and lost contact with each other. They developed separate **cultures** and adopted lifestyles that suited their **environments.** For thousands of years the ancestors of the Navajos lived as hunter-gatherers in the far north, in Canada and Alaska.

SETTLING DOWN

Although many tribes continued to gather food and hunt or fish, some Native Americans began to live in settlements and grow crops. Their homes ranged from underground pit houses and huts of mud and thatch to dwellings in cliffs. By 3500 B.C., a plentiful supply of fish in the Pacific Ocean and in rivers had enabled people to settle in large coastal villages from Alaska to Washington State. In the deserts of Arizona more than two thousand years later, farmers constructed hundreds of miles of **irrigation** canals to carry water to their crops.

In the Ohio River valley between 700 B.C. and A.D. 500, people of the Adena and Hopewell cultures built clusters of large burial mounds, such as the Serpent Mound in Ohio, which survives today. In the Mississippi **floodplains**, the native peoples formed complex societies. They created mud and thatch temples on top of flat earth pyramids. Their largest town, Cahokia, in Illinois, contained more than one hundred mounds and may have been home to thirty thousand people.

Scientists who study languages think the ancestors of the Navajos began to leave their homelands in the north around A.D. 1000 and did not arrive in the Southwest until the fifteenth century. Other scientists think the migration may have been slightly earlier.

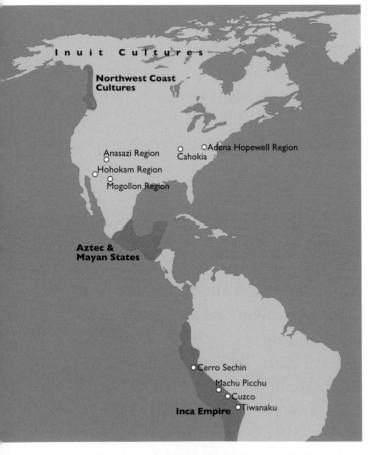

This map highlights some of the main early Native American cultures.

CONTACT WITH EUROPEANS

Around A.D. 1500, European ships reached North America. The first explorers were the Spanish. Armed with guns and riding horses, they took over land and forced the Native Americans to work for them. The Spanish were followed by the British, Dutch, and French, who were looking for land to settle and for opportunities to trade.

The Navajos acquired sheep and horses from the Spanish and became shepherds with large flocks. They began to spread out across New Mexico and Arizona.

A Navajo desert home in the late nineteenth century.

When Native Americans met these Europeans they came into contact with diseases, such as smallpox and measles, that they had never experienced before. At least one half of all Native Americans, and possibly many more than that, were unable to overcome these diseases and died.

Guns were also disastrous for Native Americans. At first, only the Europeans had guns, which enabled them to overcome native peoples in fights and battles. Eventually, Native American groups obtained guns and used them in conflicts with each other. Native American groups were also forced to take sides and fight in wars between the French and British.

Horses, too, had a big influence in Native American lifestyles, especially on the Great Plains. Some groups became horse breeders and traders. People were able to travel greater distances and began to hunt buffalo on horseback. Soon horses became central to Plains trade and social life.

At the end of the 1700s, people of European descent began to migrate over the Appalachian Mountains, looking for new land to farm and exploit. By the middle of the nineteenth century, they had reached the west coast of North America. This expansion was disastrous for Native Americans.

RESERVATION LIFE

Many native peoples were pressured into moving onto **reservations** to the west. The biggest of these reservations later became the U.S. state of Oklahoma. Native Americans who tried to remain in their homelands were attacked and defeated.

In 1848, the United States acquired New Mexico and Arizona. As new white settlers moved in and forts were built, the Navajos began to fight back. In 1863, the U.S. Army destroyed Navajo houses and crops and killed their sheep and horses to starve the Navajos. The Navajos surrendered, but were imprisoned until 1868, when those who survived moved to a reservation in one small part of their homeland.

New laws in the United States and Canada took away most of the control Native Americans had over their lives. They were expected to give up their cultures and adopt the ways and habits of white Americans. It became a crime to practice their traditional religions. Children were taken from their homes and placed in **boarding schools**, where they were forbidden to speak their native languages.

Despite this **persecution**, many Native Americans clung on to their cultures through the first half of the twentieth century. The Society of American Indians was founded in 1911 and its campaign for U.S. citizenship for Native Americans was successful in 1924. Other Native American organizations were formed to promote traditional cultures and to campaign politically for Native American rights.

A family in a Navajo camp at the time the 1930 U.S. census was taken.

THE ROAD TO SELF-GOVERNMENT

Despite these campaigns, Native Americans on reservations endured **poverty** and very low standards of living. Many of them moved away to work and live in cities, where they hoped life would be better. In most cases, they found life just as difficult. They not only faced **discrimination** and **prejudice** but also could not compete successfully for jobs against more established ethnic groups.

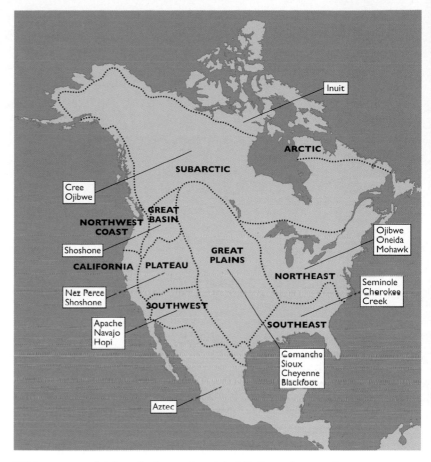

This map of North America highlights the main Native American cultural groups, along with the smaller groups, or tribes, featured in this series of books.

In the 1970s, the American Indian Movement (AIM) organized large protests that attracted attention worldwide. They highlighted the problems of unemployment, discrimination, and poverty that Native Americans experienced in North America.

The AIM protests led to changes in policy. Some new laws protected the civil rights of Native Americans, while other laws allowed tribal governments to be formed. Today, tribal governments have a wide range of powers. They operate large businesses and run their own schools and health care.

Chapter 1

LAND AND ORIGINS

LAND OF THE NAVAJOS

The Navajos are a North American native people, most of whom now live on the Navajo Reservation, which covers large portions of northeastern Arizona, southeastern Utah, and northwestern New Mexico. Numbering more than 200,000, they are the largest reservation-based Indian **nation** in North America. Only the Cherokees have more tribal members, but they are not based on a reservation.

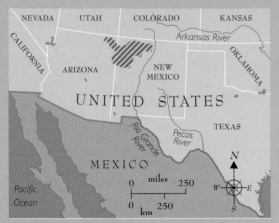

The Navajos settled in what is today New Mexico and Arizona, as shown in red, sometime between A.D. 800 and 1400.

NAVAJO ORIGIN STORY

No one knows exactly how or when Navajos and other Native Americans came to the Americas, but like many ancient cultures, traditional Navajos have long told a story

This 1873 photo of a Navajo woman with her child was taken at their home in Canyon de Chelly. Today, Canyon de Chelly is part of a national monument within the Navajo Nation.

Monument Valley, a famous landmark in the desert country of the Southwest near the Navajo Reservation. Many Western movies have been filmed in Monument Valley.

to explain their origins. Navajos believe they have passed through three previous worlds to the present fourth one, which they call the Glittering World. In each of the previous worlds, a lack of harmony among the inhabitants caused them to leave. Living in harmony with the world — and with other Navajos — is an important part of Navajo culture.

NAVAJO NAMES

Navajo is thought to be a word from the Zuni Pueblo Indian language, meaning "enemy." The Navajo word for themselves is *Dene,* meaning "the people." In 1969, the Navajo Tribal Council officially adopted the name "Navajo Nation."

Navajo Words

Here is how some ordinary Navajo words that helped win a war are pronounced. They are from the *Navajo Code Talkers' Dictionary* used in World War II. (See "Navajo Code Talkers" on page 37). Because printing Navajo words properly requires specially shaped letters, only the pronunciations are given.

Pronunciation	English
wol-la-chee	ant
be-la-sana	apple
shush	bear
ba-goshi	cow
chindi	devil
ah-jah	ear
ah-nah	eye
ah-tad	girl

11

HISTORY

Chapter 2

LIFE IN THE NEW LAND

Navajos have proven to be one of the most marvelously adaptable people in the world. Their adjustment to life in the desert Southwest is an example of that.

Before coming to the Southwest, the Navajos were hunter-gatherers. The men hunted, while the women gathered nuts, berries, wild onions, and other food. When the Navajos arrived in the Southwest, their culture was still similar to that of their close relatives, the Apaches. In fact, the early Spanish explorers of the region in the 1500s and 1600s could barely tell Navajos apart from the Apaches, who spoke a similar language.

PUEBLO PEOPLES AND THE NAVAJOS

Navajos apparently entered the Southwest at about the time of changes in the great Anasazi civilization of cliff dwellers. Partly because of a severe **drought** in the late 1300s, the Anasazis moved their farming communities to areas with more dependable water supplies near rivers and became known as the Pueblo people.

Those Pueblo people had a great impact on the Navajos, teaching them

This woodcut shows Pueblo Indian farmers in New Mexico watching over their farm fields. The Pueblos remain among the most skillful dry farmers in the world.

farming. Later, when the Spanish introduced sheep and the Pueblos learned to weave blankets and clothing, they passed those skills on to the Navajos.

From the Spanish, the Navajos acquired sheep, soon becoming expert shepherds with huge flocks. All of these new skills — farming, herding, and weaving — brought great changes to the Navajo way of life. By the 1700s, the Navajos were distinctly different from their Apache neighbors.

Navajos learned from the Pueblos that before wool can be woven into rugs on a **loom**, it must first be spun into wool thread.

Anasazi Ruins

In Navajo and Apache culture, all things having to do with the dead are avoided, so Navajos did not disturb the magnificent cliff palaces the Anasazi people had left behind. They left them in the same condition as when the Anasazi people had walked away from them.

Those spectacular ruins would have been available for scientific study if the Americans who discovered them in the late nineteenth century had not **looted** them of their pottery and virtually everything else that could be carried away. Scientists in the twentieth century were left to dig in the trash heaps of the Anasazis to try to learn about them.

This Anasazi cliff village, at the Navajo National Monument, was built sometime between the years 1250 and 1300.

Edward S. Curtis took this photo of Navajos, calling it *Out of the Darkness*. Curtis was the most famous photographer of Native Americans of the late nineteenth and early twentieth centuries, taking thousands of pictures **documenting** Native life.

CONFLICT WITH THE COLONIZERS

By the late 1500s, the Spanish had conquered much of Mexico, but the Navajos, in today's northwestern New Mexico, were too far away from areas of Spanish exploration to be much affected by it. When the Spanish began settling in New Mexico in 1598, however, Navajos soon began to feel their impact.

Throughout the 1600s and 1700s, the Spanish made slave raids against the Navajos, stealing the women and children and killing the men. To meet this threat, the Navajos stole horses from the Spanish and became expert horsemen. By the late 1600s, Navajos themselves were raiding Spanish ranches, stealing their horses, sheep, and cattle, and making Spanish attacks against them more difficult.

This photo of a Navajo man was taken in about 1880. Navajos speak a southern Athabascan language, part of the large Dene language family in North America.

14

The Spanish never conquered the Navajos. When, however, the United States defeated Mexico in a war in 1848 and acquired New Mexico and Arizona as territories, Navajo life changed dramatically. Americans soon built forts in Navajo country, and settlers began pouring into the Southwest. The Navajos, a proud, freedom-loving people, soon found themselves in conflict with a great military power, one that was determined to force its will on native people.

DESTROYING A HOMELAND

Conflicts with the Americans soon arose over grazing rights. The soldiers at the forts seized land for their animals to graze on around their forts. This pushed some Navajos off their land; when the Indians stood up for themselves, fighting broke out.

Different People, Different Attitudes
It is better to feed the Indians, than to fight them.
William Carr Lane, Governor of New Mexico Territory, 1852

Chastisement [of the Navajos] must be more severe; they must be well punished and thoroughly humbled.
James L. Collins, New Mexico Indian Superintendent, 1859

An Indian is a more watchful and a more wary animal than a deer. He must be hunted with skill.
U.S. Brigadier General James H. Carleton, 1863

A Horse Race Becomes a Massacre

In 1861, about five hundred Navajos gathered for a horse race with the soldiers at Fort Canby in Navajo country. The soldiers cheated by cutting the reins of the Navajo horses, causing them to break during the race. When the Navajos demanded their money back, the soldiers attacked them, killing about forty Navajos. As U.S. Army Captain Nicholas Hodt described the scene at the time:

"The Navajos, squaws [women], and children ran in all directions and were shot and bayoneted. I succeeded in forming about twenty men. . . . I then marched out to the east side of the post; there I saw a soldier murdering two little children and a woman. I halloed immediately to the soldier to stop. He looked up, but did not obey my order."

An 1845 photo of Kit Carson, who led a devastating U.S. Army operation against the Navajos in the 1860s. The government encouraged civilians and other Indians to raid the Navajo homeland during this campaign.

To make matters worse, the United States was soon torn apart by its own **Civil War**. With Americans from the North and South slaughtering each other by the hundreds of thousands in brutal battles, the value of any life seemed cheap. American attitudes toward Indians hardened as well.

The U.S. Army decided to end Navajo resistance by destroying their homeland. That job was given to Colonel Kit Carson, who disagreed with the policy but carried it out anyway. In 1863, Colonel Carson led an army through the Navajo homeland, burning houses, destroying crops, killing sheep and horses, and even chopping down fruit trees.

A LONG WALK TO DEATH

By 1864, several thousand Navajos had fled to remote areas farther west, while about eight thousand starving Navajos had surrendered to the U.S. Army. They were forced to walk about 300 miles (480 kilometers), all the way across New Mexico, to the Bosque Redondo prison camp in the "Navajo Long Walk."

The Navajos were kept prisoners at Bosque Redondo, under terrible conditions, until 1868, when they were finally allowed to **negotiate** their only **treaty** with the U.S. government. The treaty allowed them to return to their homeland, but by that time, many had died of disease in the prison camp.

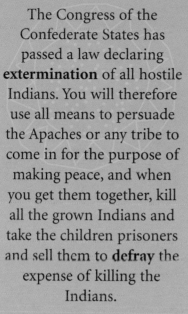

> The Congress of the Confederate States has passed a law declaring **extermination** of all hostile Indians. You will therefore use all means to persuade the Apaches or any tribe to come in for the purpose of making peace, and when you get them together, kill all the grown Indians and take the children prisoners and sell them to **defray** the expense of killing the Indians.
>
> *Lieutenant Colonel John Robert Baker, Confederate Civil War commander in Arizona and New Mexico, 1862*

An 1874 photo of Manuelito (1818–1894). A famous Navajo leader, he signed the Navajo treaty with the United States in 1868.

The surviving Navajos walked back to their destroyed homeland a defeated people. They would never again be at war with the Americans.

RESERVATION LIFE

When the Navajos returned home to northwestern New Mexico from Bosque Redondo in 1868, the U.S. government provided them with sheep to begin rebuilding their flocks and with food to support them for ten years. However, the treaty of 1868 reduced Navajo Nation land to 10 percent of what it once was. Over the next few decades, the United States increased the size of the reservation several times, but it remains much smaller than the old homeland.

Navajo students in the Carlisle Indian School Library. This off-reservation boarding school was located in Pennsylvania, all the way across the continent from the Navajo homeland.

FORCED CHANGES

One of the cruelest parts of reservation life was forcing Navajo children to attend boarding schools far from home. The boarding schools tried to turn Navajo children into white people, forcing them to learn the Christian religion and speak English. The children had to do all the labor at the schools — the cleaning, cooking, and farming that provided the food. In the 1930s, day schools on the reservation began replacing the boarding schools, and Navajo children were able to live at home while attending school.

Navajos had never had a centralized, national government. After oil was discovered on the reservation in 1921, however, the

Drilling for oil on the Navajo Reservation in 1958, these workers add a drill stem section to a pipe. Payments for mineral leases help support the tribal government.

A tribal council meeting near Window Rock on the Navajo Reservation in Arizona in 1938. Like many Native American nations, the Navajos were forced to create a centralized government by the United States.

U.S. government forced them to form a government because it needed one to sign oil **leases**.

A DEADLY DISCOVERY

In the 1950s, uranium was discovered on the reservation. The Navajos mined the deadly **radioactive** material, which is used to make atomic bombs, but were not told about its health risks. Many became ill and died of cancer. In 1984, the U.S. government provided money to begin cleaning up the uranium poisoning on the reservation and in 1990 paid money to the surviving Navajo victims of radiation poisoning.

Navajo Stock Reduction

In the 1930s, when Lake Meade, the main water supply for southern California, began filling up with **silt**, the government blamed it on overgrazing by livestock on the nearby Navajo Reservation. The U.S. government shot hundreds of thousands of sheep, goats, and horses, leaving their bodies to rot and the Navajos in poverty. Scientists later found that silting in Lake Meade had nothing to do with Navajo livestock grazing.

Chapter 3

TRADITIONAL WAY OF LIFE

TRADITIONAL LIFESTYLES

Navajo families are matriarchal, meaning that a woman, usually the grandmother, is the head of the household. Men who marry her daughters become part of the household. When a son marries, he goes to live with his wife's family. Navajo girls grow up learning that they will one day be responsible for leading their family.

Made of wood, the typical traditional Navajo house is called a hogan. A hole in the center of the roof allows smoke to escape from the cooking fire. The doorway always faces the rising sun in the east. Navajos typically build a hogan in a valley for their

This family stands outside their hogan near the south rim of the Grand Canyon. The photo was taken early in the twentieth century.

winter home and another one near their mountain pastures, which they live in during the summer months.

During the nineteenth century, Navajos developed distinctive styles of clothing. Women favored colorful blouses and skirts, while men wore jeans, boots, and colorful shirts. A black hat became very popular for men. Both men and women wore silver and turquoise jewelry, a distinctive Navajo tradition that is still very popular.

Navajo Silversmithing

Navajos first learned how to make jewelry out of silver from a Mexican silversmith at Fort Defiance, a U.S. Army outpost built in the middle of the nineteenth century in Navajo country. Requiring great skill in hammering and shaping the precious metal, silversmithing is a delicate art. Navajos later added beautiful turquoise stones to create a distinctive jewelry prized by collectors all over the world.

Above: A woman displays her turquoise jewelry at the Navajo Nation Parade. Tourists also buy Navajo turquoise jewelry, adding income to the Navajo economy. Right: This silver belt buckle was made by pouring melted metal into a sand mold.

Navajo Weaving

Navajo women first learned how to weave wool from the Pueblo Indians. Working with the Spanish merino sheep wool, they soon began fashioning some of the most beautiful blankets in the world.

This weaver is carding wool, making the wool strands all lie in one direction. She is sitting inside a trading post while working at her task.

This photo, taken sometime during the first half of the twentieth century, shows women weaving blankets from wool on outdoor looms near their home. The outdoors provided more coolness and light for their work than their hogan.

Many families live outside during the summers since the Navajo homeland is mostly desert. People cook and sleep outside, and women set up their weaving looms outdoors, under a pole structure with a roof made of brush to provide shade. Girls learn how to weave from their mother, grandmother, and aunts.

LIFE WITH SHEEP

The Navajo homeland proved nearly perfect for raising sheep, which provided Navajo families with food (**mutton** stew is a favorite) and fine wool for weaving blankets and clothing. It's an occupation the entire family can participate in, with men and children tending flocks and women weaving, cooking, and maintaining the household.

In the late nineteenth century, trading post operators began selling Navajo blankets, putting them in catalogs that soon made them famous. Today, Navajo weavers offer their blankets each year at a famous sale at Crownpoint, New Mexico, that brings buyers and collectors from all over the world.

Many Navajo boys and girls of all ages spend their summers on horseback, helping move sheep to summer **pastures** in the mountains and then staying there to tend the flocks. In the fall, men and boys hunt deer in the mountains. Women tend the gardens and peach orchards, growing vegetables and fruit to add to the family diet.

In this 1948 photo, a young sheepherder takes the family flock out to graze at Window Rock, on the Navajo Reservation in Arizona.

23

A Belief in Harmony

Traditional Navajo values place great importance on living in harmony. Learning about living in harmony begins with the Navajo creation story, in which Navajos have fled three previous worlds because life got too far out of balance. To "walk in beauty" with one's surroundings is more important for Navajos than trying to do many other things, like getting rich. Navajos who acquire wealth are expected to share it with their relatives. Bad behavior for a Navajo is "to act like he doesn't have any relatives." Thus, as with most other Indian cultures, individuals are taught from an early age to think about the welfare of the group.

This medicine man, a Navajo singer, wears a traditional necklace. This photo was taken in about 1900 in New Mexico.

Healing Ceremonies

According to tradition, being out of harmony causes illness. When that happens, Navajos consult experts, called hand tremblers or crystal gazers, who can tell the nature of the illness and recommend the right healing ceremony to restore the patient to harmony. A **medicine man**, called a singer, will then conduct the ceremony.

The purpose of a ceremony is to restore the patient to harmony. As an example, one of the most famous ceremonies is the Enemy Way Ceremony for Navajo soldiers returning from war. The ceremony cleanses the soldier of the **contamination** of death and of other evils from fighting.

A Navajo singer shown during a healing ceremony. More than one thousand different sand painting designs are used in the many different kinds of ceremonies; during a lifetime of study, one singer can learn only a few of the ceremonies.

SONGS AND SAND PAINTINGS

Long, complicated **rituals**, Navajo healing ceremonies last several days and require many people as helpers, singers, and dancers. The principal singers must study for many years to memorize the songs and sand paintings of just one ceremony.

A Navajo singer prepares a sand painting on the ground. Making sand paintings requires years of study to learn the many different patterns used in just one ceremony.

Though there are many different kinds of ceremonies, there are only a small number of singers to perform them. The ceremonies require such long study that few medicine men are able to learn more than one or two. Some ceremonies have been lost when the only singer who still knew them died.

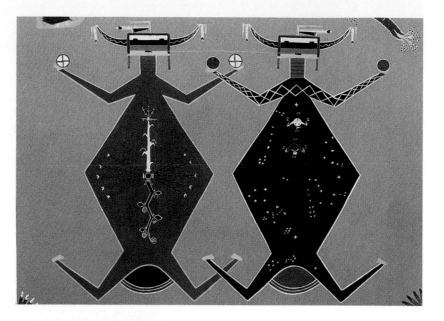

This bold sand painting represents Mother Earth and Father Sky. The image can also be turned upside down.

Hosteen Klah (1867-1937)

In the early twentieth century, Navajo Hosteen Klah became the most famous ceremony singer and weaver. Before becoming the principal singer for one of the longest, most complicated ceremonies, he had to study with older singers for more than twenty-five years to learn all the songs and sand paintings of that ritual. At the end of that nine-day ceremony, he was recognized as one of the greatest singers on the Navajo Reservation. He later caused **controversy** by using images from sand paintings as patterns in his weaving. Other medicine men thought that sand paintings should not be for public display.

The sand paintings used in the ceremonies are temporary, made on the ground with different colors of sand inside the family hogan. The person being healed sits in the middle of the sand painting, and the illness is transferred to the painting, which is then destroyed.

THE SUPPORT OF THE CLAN

Other ceremonies celebrate changes in life, such as a girl's **puberty** ceremony, called a *kinaalda*. All of the girl's relatives participate in the celebration of her entry into womanhood, one of the most important events in her life. The kinaalda features songs and dances and lasts for several days.

Ceremonies are very expensive because the family hosting one must feed many people for up to nine days. They must also pay the principal singer a large fee, often in **livestock**. Deciding to hold a ceremony for someone is a serious decision, requiring the help and support of many relatives. Because so many family members and community members are involved, Navajo ceremonies also help create positive connections between people in the community.

Children get their clan membership from their parents. These clans spread out across the Navajo Nation, giving people extended family across the land. Clan membership carries responsibilities to and for other clan members. Since their traditional culture had no government, clan relationships were — and remain — very important.

This woman is participating in the Spring Snow Ceremony in the mid-1960s. She is in the Luckachukai Mountains on the Navajo Reservation, along the border between Arizona and New Mexico.

Earth and Sky

Navajo stories feature both the local landscape and the sky above. Here are two examples.

SPIDER ROCK

Spider Rock is a tall, narrow rock formation that rises from the floor of the Canyon de Chelly in Arizona. The Navajos believe that the top of the rock is the home of Spider Woman, a supernatural being who taught weaving to the Navajos.

Once a young Navajo was hunting in the canyon when he saw an enemy from another tribe. The young man ran around looking for a hiding place. Finally he reached the bottom of Spider Rock. There was a rope of silk hanging down from the top of the rock, so he quickly climbed up it to safety, and found

Spider Woman at home. The young man stayed there until it was safe to go down again.

The story of Spider Woman and her silk rope is also used to scare naughty Navajo children. They are told that Spider Woman will come down her rope, carry them back up to the top of the rock, and eat them.

Spider Rock formed more than two hundred million years ago. Around it in the cliff walls that surround the canyon, Navajo people used to live in caves they carved out of the rock.

CREATING THE HEAVENS

In the Navajo story, the earliest people wanted more light, so the goddess First Woman and the god Fire Man helped them. The people were told to carve the sun and moon out of large quartz rocks. The sun rock was given a blue turquoise mask to produce light and heat. The moon rock was decorated with white shell and carried coolness and moisture.

After the sun and moon had been carved, there were many small pieces of quartz lying on the ground. Fire Man shot fire arrows into the sky, and their trails formed a ladder. Then Fire Man took the pieces of quartz up the ladder and placed them in the sky where First Woman decided they should go. Each group of stars, or constellation, was put there as a symbol of Navajo law, but today only medicine men know their meanings.

Orion (above) and the Pleiades (left) are two star groups in the night sky. The Navajos call Orion "the Big Slender One." He protects the Pleiades, who are a group of children. They are called "the Planters" by the Navajos because they appear at the time of the year when crops should be planted.

NAVAJO LIFE TODAY

Chapter 4

LITERATURE AND ART

Through literature and art, Navajos may very well have done more than any other tribe in expressing what it means to see the world through the eyes of their culture. Navajo author and storyteller Vee Browne has won awards for her children's versions of traditional Navajo stories. Beautifully illustrated, the books tell of the adventures of Navajo cultural heroes with names like Monster Slayer and Born of Water.

Navajos have also produced many great poets. The songs of the healing ceremonies are works of beautiful poetry. Handed down from **generation** to generation, they were created so long ago that no one knows the names of the people who produced them. These songs were composed before Navajos had a written version of their language, and for many generations the only way to learn them has been to memorize them by studying with a singer, listening to the singer chant the songs.

One modern Navajo who has become famous for expressing what it means to be Navajo in works of poetry is Luci Tapahonso, a literature professor at the University of Arizona.

Wearing traditional dress and moccasins, the Blue Earth Singers perform onstage in Gallup, New Mexico. Song, poetry, and art remain important in Navajo culture.

This painting by Nelson Tsosie is titled *Silver Horizons*. Tsosie uses images from Navajo life in both his paintings and his sculptures.

Another Navajo professor at the same university who has become famous for his writing is Irvin Morris. His book, *From the Glittering World*, is used in college courses to learn about the Navajo view of the world.

Navajos have also produced some of the most famous Indian painters, including R. C. Gorman, Carl Nelson Gorman, and Paul Apodaca. The Navajo homeland is a strikingly beautiful place that comes alive in the work of these great painters.

Diné College

In 1969, the Navajo people became the first Indian nation to have its own college, originally called Navajo Nation Community College and now called Diné College. Owned and operated by the Navajo Nation, it now has several branch **campuses**. The main campus, at Tsaile, sits on top of Canyon de Chelly, one of the most beautiful places in North America. Following the lead of the Navajos, about two dozen tribes now have their own colleges.

THE NAVAJO NATION

When a formal government for the Navajo people was being created in the 1920s, one problem that had to be overcome was the great distances that separated Navajos from one another. Navajos were a **rural** people, a nation of widely scattered shepherding families. The plan that was adopted created more than one hundred local units called Chapter Houses. Today, the Chapter Houses are still the basic foundation for the Navajo Nation government.

The Navajo Nation Council is the national **legislature** of the Navajo people, who also elect a president to lead the Navajo Nation. The capital of the Navajo Nation is at Window Rock, in northeastern Arizona. The town is named for a famous rock formation that has a big hole in it, like a window.

The Navajo Nation Tribal Police help to maintain law and order in the nation, and the Navajos have their own court system. The most serious crimes, however, are still investigated by the U.S. Federal Bureau of Investigation (FBI).

The famous Window Rock, near the Navajo Nation capital at Window Rock, Arizona.

Hubbell Trading Post

The Hubbell Trading Post is now a National Historic Site on the Navajo Reservation. Trading posts were part general store, part post office, part **pawn shop**, and always a gathering place for Navajos from all around the area. The trading post operators would write letters for Navajos, make loans by taking their turquoise and silver jewelry in pawn, serve as counselors for legal matters, and provide a variety of other services other than just operating a store.

The tribe also publishes its own newspaper, *The Navajo Times*. Several radio stations broadcast in the Navajo language, which is spoken by more than 200,000 people. With so many speakers, it is in no danger of being lost like so many other Indian languages.

THE NAVAJO RESERVATION

The Navajo Reservation lies in a high-altitude desert dotted with mountains atop the Colorado Plateau. With cold winters and hot summers, it's a rugged, dry country.

A farm at Canyon del Muerto on the Navajo Reservation in Arizona. A land of vast spaces, the reservation is so huge that homes can be quite isolated.

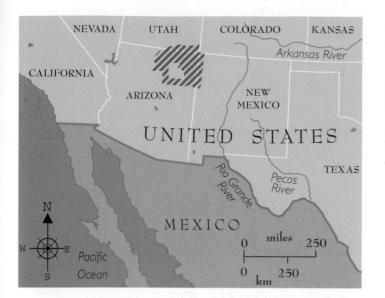

As shown in red, the current boundaries for the Navajo Reservation include land in parts of New Mexico, Arizona, and Utah. The green in the middle represents the Hopi Reservation, which is entirely surrounded by the Navajo Reservation.

The introduction of automobiles during the early twentieth century ended much of the isolation on the Navajo Reservation. However, only the main highways through the reservation are paved. Most of the reservation is still lonely backcountry, where horses can get to places cars cannot go.

Much of the reservation still does not have things that most Americans take for granted, like electricity. People often still use fires to prepare food, and many still depend on their livestock to provide much of that food. Navajo children frequently take long bus rides to school.

A woman demonstrates how to make fry bread over an open fire. Many Navajo women prefer outdoor cooking.

Jobs on the Reservation

The federal and tribal governments are now the biggest employers on the Navajo Reservation, but stock raising and farming still provide many jobs. The tribe also operates an electronics business and a sawmill.

Navajo Scientist

Fred Begay was born in 1932 to Navajo and Ute parents who were native healers. He was taken from his reservation at the age of ten and trained as a farmer. After serving in the U.S. Air Force in the Korean War, he studied physics (the science of energy and matter) at the University of New Mexico.

Begay joined the Los Alamos National Laboratory in 1971 to study space physics. He now uses his skills in physics to conduct research into ways of providing environmentally safe power.

Fred Begay has worked with the Navajo government on scientific matters and he has encouraged interest in science in Navajo middle schools. In his studies he has made many connections between modern science and traditional Navajo beliefs and healing.

Fred Begay in 2004, when he was elected to the New York Academy of Sciences for his contribution to physics research.

Tourism is not big business, although the Navajos own some campgrounds and sell fishing and hunting permits. There are many art and craft shops, and most Navajo families include people who make extra money from traditional skills such as weaving and making silver jewelry.

Money from mining companies, who pay to exploit Navajo land, is a large portion of the Nation's income. In 2004, the Diné Development Corporation was formed to promote and help create Navajo business enterprises.

EDUCATION

Many of the 150 public schools on the reservation are substandard, and high numbers of students drop out of high school. However, the Navajo Preparatory School, Inc., at Farmington, New Mexico, is controlled by the Navajo Nation, and it takes only talented students who intend to go on to colleges and universities. As well as demanding high academic standards from its students, the school offers courses in Navajo culture.

Children in a classroom at an elementary school on the reservation. Children are taught in Navajo as well as in English.

HEALTH PROBLEMS

With around half the population living in poverty, the Navajo Reservation has high suicide and alcoholism rates. Other problems are diabetes, which is four times as common as in the United States in general, and cancers caused by uranium waste from mining.

The Navajos run their own health centers, which are now built to include rooms for traditional healers to practice in. There are plans to develop a native medical school at Shiprock, New Mexico.

Navajo Code Talkers

During World War II (1939– 1945), more than four hundred Navajos served in the United States Marine Corps, sending radio messages on the battlefield in a secret Navajo-language code. The Marines recruited twenty-nine Navajos to invent the code in 1942. It was so successful that the Japanese were never able to crack it. In 1982, U.S. President Ronald Reagan honored the surviving Navajo code talkers.

These Navajo code talkers in World War II were among the first groups of Marines to land on the Japanese-held island of Saipan in the western Pacific Ocean in 1944.

A young airman jokes with several surviving Navajo Code Talkers at a book signing in Albuquerque, New Mexico.

Chapter 5

CURRENT NAVAJO ISSUES

The Navajos and Hopis are arguing over a portion of the Navajo Reservation in northeastern Arizona that the two tribes once shared. Some Navajo families have been ordered to leave that land, which has created ongoing problems between the two nations, problems they have difficulty resolving.

URANIUM POLLUTION

Although uranium mining stopped in Monument Valley in 1969, radioactive materials and waste still cause serious health problems. Drinking water for 30 percent of the Navajo population contains radioactive substances, and even some of the rocks the Navajos use to build their homes are radioactive. Now the Environmental Protection Agency is trying to improve conditions for the Navajos. In 2008, it began to clean up water supplies, homes, and five hundred old uranium mills.

Navajo School Board members march to celebrate the opening of the National Museum of the American Indian in Washington D.C.

Looking to the Future

The Navajo Nation has started a number of programs to provide jobs. One is a huge agricultural irrigation project in the San Juan River Valley in New Mexico that is turning desert into cropland.

For many years, the Navajo Nation opposed building any **casinos** as many other tribes in New Mexico and Arizona have done. Recently, however, they have decided that the income and jobs casinos provide outweigh the disadvantages. The first casino, which employs 320 people, opened in 2008. It was followed by a second casino in 2010, and there are plans for more.

A Living Culture

Navajos are fortunate to still live in their ancestral homeland, unlike many other Indian peoples who were removed to Indian Territory (now Oklahoma). This has helped them to maintain their culture. They are entering the twenty-first century with confidence and pride — and with more control of their own destiny than many previous generations.

Fireman apprentice Andrea Barney says a Navajo prayer aboard the aircraft carrier USS *Harry S. Truman* as part of a celebration of Native American and Alaskan heritage.

TIMELINE

A.D. 800 to 1400	Navajos migrate out of the far north and arrive in the Southwest; they settle in desert land that the Pueblo peoples have deserted because of lack of water.
1400s to 1600s	Expert farmers, the Pueblo Indians in the Southwest greatly influence the hunting and gathering Navajos, who learn how to grow crops.
1600s and 1700s	Spanish settlers in New Mexico make slave raids against the Navajos; the Navajos fight back by raiding Spanish ranches. The Navajos become expert shepherds and learn how to weave wool from the Pueblo Indians using wool from Spanish sheep.
late 1700s	Spanish make peace with the Comanches and Navajos.
1810–20	Mexican Revolution throws the Southwest region into chaos.
1848	United States acquires New Mexico and Arizona, and white settlers pour into the region.
1851	U.S. Army builds Fort Defiance in Navajo country, setting off disputes about grazing rights in the area near the fort. Fighting breaks out.
1861	U.S. Army kills about forty Navajos at Fort Canby.
1863	Colonel Kit Carson's U.S. troops destroy Navajo homes, crops, and animals; several thousand Navajos flee westward; eight thousand surrender to the U.S. Army.
1864	Navajo Long Walk: Navajos are forced to march to Bosque Redondo prison camp, where many die of disease.
1868	First and only U.S. treaty with Navajos allows survivors of Bosque Redondo to return to a reservation on their homeland in northwestern New Mexico; Navajo land has been reduced to 10 percent of its original size.

1882	Hopi Reservation is created within the Navajo Reservation.
late 1800s and early 1900s	U.S. government increases the size of Navajo Reservation; sends Navajo children to government boarding schools.
1921	Oil discovered on the Navajo Reservation.
1923	U.S. government forces Navajos to form a national government, so oil leases can be made with oil companies.
1930s	Silting of Lake Meade is wrongly blamed on Navajo overgrazing. Day schools begin to replace boarding schools.
1951	U.S. companies discover uranium on Navajo Reservation.
1962	A Navajo-Hopi Joint Use Area is created.
1960s and 1970s	Native American protests change government policy toward self-government and education.
1969	Navajo Tribal Council officially adopts the name "Navajo Nation." Navajo Community College (now Diné College) opens.
1974	Congress tries to force thousands of Navajos to move from Navajo-Hopi Joint Use Area, touching off protests.
1984	U.S. government provides money to clean up uranium poisoning on the Navajo Reservation.
1990	Congress provides money to Navajo victims of uranium poisoning.
2004	Diné Development Corporation is formed to create new jobs.
2008	Environmental Protection Agency begins a 5-year uranium pollution cleanup program. First casino on the reservation opens.
2010	Second casino opens.

GLOSSARY

ancestors: people from whom an individual or group is descended.

boarding schools: places where students must live at the school.

campus: the grounds of a university or college.

casinos: buildings with slot machines and other gambling games.

census: an official record of facts about a population.

Civil War: war between northern and southern U.S. states that took place between 1861 and 1865.

contamination: the process of becoming unclean or stained.

controversy: long-lasting, public disagreement.

culture: the arts, beliefs, and customs that make up a people's way of life.

defray: to reduce.

discrimination: unjust treatment usually because of a person's race or sex.

documenting: recording something in writing or photographs.

drought: a shortage of water, usually caused by low rainfall.

environment: objects and conditions all around that affect living things and communities.

extermination: the killing of everyone or everything.

floodplain: the area of land beside a river or stream that is covered with water during a flood.

generation: a group of people born around the same time, or one step in the line of descent of a family.

ice age: a period of time when the earth is very cold and lots of water in the oceans turns to ice.

irrigation: any system for watering the land to grow plants.

leases: written agreements to rent land or buildings. Mineral leases allow people to have their land mined without giving up actual ownership.

legislature: a group of people elected to make or pass laws.

livestock: farm animals.

loom: a frame that holds wool threads to be woven into a blanket or other material.

looted: stolen.

medicine man: a healer and spiritual leader.

migration: movement from one place to another.

mutton: the meat that comes from adult sheep.

nation: people who have their own customs, laws, and land separate from other nations or people.

negotiate: to work with others to come to an agreement.

pasture: land on which grazing animals feed.

pawn shop: a store where a person can leave a valuable object in return for a loan of money. The object is left as a promise that the person will return the money.

persecution: treating someone or a certain group of people badly over a period of time.

poverty: the state of being poor.

prejudice: dislike or injustice that is not based on reason or experience.

puberty: the time of physical changes in the human body when a girl becomes a woman or a boy becomes a man.

radioactive: giving off energy in the form of rays. Being near radioactive material can make a person very sick.

reservation: land set aside by the U.S. government for specific Native American tribes to live on.

rituals: systems of special ceremonies, usually spiritual ones.

rural: of the countryside.

silt: material carried along by running water which eventually sinks to the bottom of the water.

treaty: an agreement among two or more nations.

MORE RESOURCES

WEBSITES:

http://www.angelfire.com/rock3/countryboy79/ navajo_astronomy.html

Descriptions and meanings of the Navajo constellations (star groups) and their links to Navajo string games.

http://www.bigorrin.org/navajo_kids.htm

Online Navajo Indian Fact Sheet For Kids in question-and-answer form with useful links.

http://www.desertusa.com/mag08/jan08/navajoblankets.html

A page about Navajo blankets and weaving on the DesertUSA website.

http://www.imagesofarizona.com/dejolie/leroyindex.shtml

Navajo photographer LeRoy DeJolie's images of Navajo Nation Fair.

http://www.meredith.edu/nativeam/navajo.htm

Choose from many topics of Navajo culture and history, learn about them, and answer questions. Lots of photos and lists of places where you can find out more.

http://www.native-languages.org/navajo.htm

Links to online Navajo language resources.

http://www.native-languages.org/navajo-legends.htm

Many links to Navajo legends and traditional stories and to books on Navajo mythology.

http://www.nps.gov/history/museum/exhibits/hutr/index.html

An online collection of historic portraits of Navajo people.

http://www.windows.ucar.edu/tour/link=/mythology/ northamerican_culture.html

Visit the links to read Navajo stories about the stars, Earth, and various gods.

DVD:

Navajo Code Talkers (In Search of History). A&E Home Video, 2006.

BOOKS:

Browne, Vee. *The Stone Cutter and the Navajo Maiden*. Salina Bookshelf, Inc., 2008.

Bruchac, Joseph. *Code Talker: A Novel About the Navajo Marines of World War Two*. Speak, 2006.

Craats, Rennay. *The Navajo (American Indian Art and Culture)*. Chelsea House Publications, 2004.

Cunningham, Kevin, and Peter Benoit. *The Navajo (True Books)*. Children's Press, 2011.

Flood, Nancy Bo. *The Navajo Year: Activities for Learning and Exploring*. Salina Bookshelf, Inc., 2006.

Flood, Nancy Bo. *The Navajo Year: Walk Through Many Seasons*. Salina Bookshelf, Inc., 2006.

Gibson, Karen Bush. *Native American History for Kids: With 21 Activities*. Chicago Review Press, 2010.

King, David C. *First People*. DK Children, 2008.

Lassieur, Allison. *The Navajo: A Proud People (American Indians)*. Enslow Elementary, 2005.

Murdoch, David S. *North American Indian (DK Eyewitness Books)*. DK Children, 2005.

Niethammer, Carolyn. *Keeping the Rope Straight*. Salina Bookshelf, Inc., 2006.

Parsons-Yazzie, Evangeline. *Little Woman Warrior Who Came Home*. Salina Bookshelf, Inc., 2005.

Rosinsky, Natalie M. *The Navajo (First Reports)*. Compass Point Books, 2004.

Santella, Andrew. *Navajo Code Talkers (We the People)*. Compass Point Books, 2004.

Sonneborn, Liz. *The Navajos (Native American Histories)*. Lerner Classroom, 2007.

THINGS TO THINK ABOUT AND DO

CHANGING WITH THE TIMES

Navajos have shown great ability to adopt useful things from other people, including farming; raising horses, sheep, and goats; weaving; and making jewelry from silver (silversmithing). Write a short essay about how these things would change the everyday lives of people who had lived mostly by hunting.

YOU ARE THERE

Pretend you are a newspaper reporter in 1863. Write a short newspaper article about Colonel Kit Carson's war campaign in the Navajo homeland. Now pretend you are a Navajo and write down how you would describe the campaign to other Navajos.

NEGOTIATING A TREATY

Imagine that you are one of the Navajo leaders at Bosque Redondo negotiating the Treaty of 1868. The U.S. government wants to move the Navajos to the Great Plains in Indian Territory (now Oklahoma). Make a list of the arguments you might make for allowing Navajos to return to the Navajo homeland rather than being moved to Indian Territory.

AN ART PROJECT

Using markers, paints, crayons, or colored pencils, design your own Navajo blanket or jewelry. Research patterns and designs in other books and on the websites listed on page 44.

INDEX

Adena culture 6
Alaska 4, 5
American Indian Movement 9
Anasazi culture 12, 13
Apache people 12, 13
Apodaca, Paul 31
Asia 4

Baker, John Robert 17
Barney, Andrea 39
Begay, Fred 35
beliefs 8, 18, 24–26, 35
Bering Strait 4
Blue Earth Singers 30
Bosque Redondo 16, 17
Browne, Vee 30

Cahokia, Illinois 6
Canada 4, 5
Canyon de Chelly 10, 28, 31
Carleton, James H. 15
Carson, Kit 16
casinos 39
ceremonies 24–27
Chapter Houses 32
Cherokee people 10
civil rights 9
clans 26–27

Cliff Palace, Mesa Verde 5
climate 4, 5
clothing 21
Collins, James L. 15
cooking 34
Curtis, Edward S. 14

Diné College 31
diseases 7, 16, 19, 37

education 8, 18, 34, 36
employment 9, 35–36, 39
Enemy Way Ceremony 24
Europeans 6, 7, 13

farming 5, 12–13, 23,35
fishing 5

gathering 5, 12
Gorman, Carl Nelson 31
Gorman, R. C. 31
government 18–19, 32
guns 6, 7

healing ceremonies 24–26, 30
health care 37
Hodt, Nicholas 15
hogans 20

Hopewell culture 6
Hopi people 38
horses 6, 7, 14, 23
housing 5, 7, 8, 13, 20–21
Hubbell Trading Post 33
hunting 5, 12, 23

ice ages 4

jewelry 21

Klah, Hosteen 26

Lane, William Carr 15
language 8, 11, 12, 14, 18, 30, 33,
    36, 37
literature 30–31
livestock 13, 17, 19, 23
Long Walk 16

Manuelito 17
medicine men (singers) 24, 25,
    26, 27, 29
migration 4, 5, 6
Monument Valley 11
Morris, Irvin 31

Navajo Code Talkers 11, 37
Navajo Nation 10, 11, 32–33, 39
Navajo Reservation 10, 17, 18, 19,
    33–37, 38
    ⁙o Tribal Council 11

origin story 10–11

painters 31
poverty 9
puberty ceremony (kinaalda)
    26–27
Pueblo people 12–13, 22

reservations 8, 17, 18, 19

sand paintings 25–26
sheep 6, 13, 17, 23
silversmithing 21, 36
social life 20, 24, 26–27
Society of American Indians 8
songs 25, 26, 27, 30
Spider Rock 28
Spring Snow Ceremony 27
stories 10–11, 28-29, 30

Tapahonso, Luci 30
trade 6, 7
Tsosie, Nelson 31

uranium pollution 19, 38

war 7, 8, 15–16, 24
weaving 13, 22, 23, 26, 36
Window Rock 23, 32

Zuni people 11